Harry Styles

Published in the UK by Scholastic Children's Books, 2021
Euston House, 24 Eversholt Street, London, NW1 1DB
A division of Scholastic Limited

London ~ New York ~ Toronto ~ Sydney ~ Auckland
Mexico City ~ New Delhi ~ Hong Kong

SCHOLASTIC and associated logos are trademarks and/or
registered trademarks of Scholastic Inc.

ISBN 978 0702 30795 9

Text by Emily Hibbs © Scholastic Children's Books
Design by Cloud King Creative

A CIP catalogue record for this book is available from the British Library.

2 4 6 8 10 9 7 5 3 1

Printed and bound in the UK by Bell and Bain Ltd, Glasgow
Papers used by Scholastic Children's Books are made from wood grown in sustainable forests.

www.scholastic.co.uk

Harry Styles

100%
Unofficial
Fan book

SCHOLASTIC

CONTENTS

Introduction

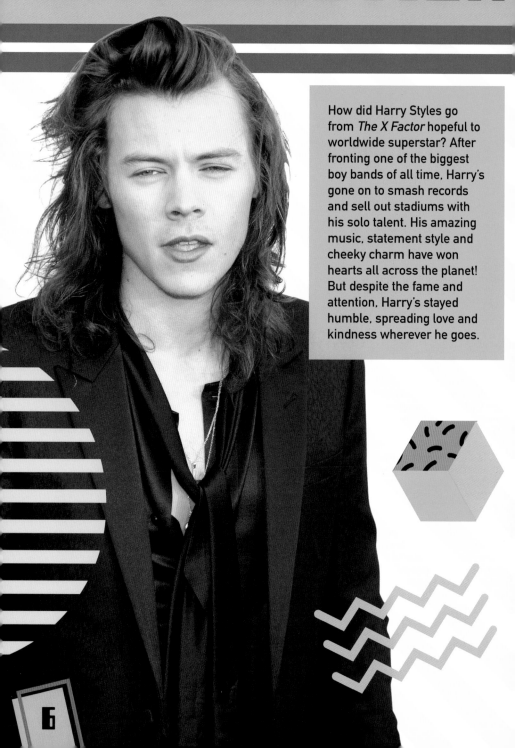

How did Harry Styles go from *The X Factor* hopeful to worldwide superstar? After fronting one of the biggest boy bands of all time, Harry's gone on to smash records and sell out stadiums with his solo talent. His amazing music, statement style and cheeky charm have won hearts all across the planet! But despite the fame and attention, Harry's stayed humble, spreading love and kindness wherever he goes.

In this book, you can get to know the real Harry. Discover his journey from a quiet English village to the top of the world, meet his musical inspirations, find out where he gets his fashion sense from and much more. Plus, try out some Styles-centric activities, from designing a new outfit for him to scribbling your own lyrics. Finally, test your superfan knowledge with the ultimate Harry Styles quiz.

Harry Styles:

FACTFILE

NAME: Harry Edward Styles

NICKNAMES:
H, Hazza, Harold

DATE OF BIRTH:
1 February 1994

BORN IN:
Worcestershire, England

FAMOUS AS:
singer, songwriter and actor

YOU CAN KEEP UP
WITH ALL THINGS
HARRY ON HIS SOCIAL
MEDIA CHANNELS.

Instagram: @harrystyles

Twitter: @Harry_Styles

STAY SAFE ONLINE

Twitter, Instagram, Snapchat, TikTok and other social media apps are great ways to stay in touch with friends and keep up to date with your favourite celebrities. However, it's important to be smart and stay safe online.

DON'T give out personal details like your full name, address or school and never request these details from anyone else.

DON'T upload photos in your school uniform, as that might allow people to pinpoint your location.

DON'T ignore an app or website's age restrictions – they have them for a reason.

DO report any comments that make you feel uncomfortable to a trusted adult.

DO remember to be respectful of other users, including those who have different opinions to you. Treat them with kindness – there are real people behind the keyboards.

HERE COMES HARRY!

Harry was born on 1 February 1994. When he was still a baby, the family moved to Holmes Chapel, Cheshire, a quiet village in the English countryside. He lived with his mum, Anne, his dad, Desmond, his big sister, Gemma, and their dog, Max.

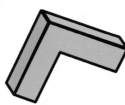

Even when he was very little, Harry had a BIG personality. He had bags of confidence and made friends with just about everybody at school. He could be loud and talkative but was also caring and loved to make other people happy.

When he was seven years old, Harry's mum and dad separated. It was a tough time for Harry and Gemma, but their parents made sure they felt safe and supported. Anne filled their family home with love and showed Harry how strong a person could be.

MUSIC ALL AROUND

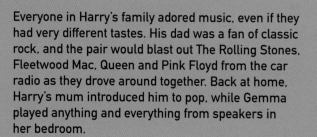

Everyone in Harry's family adored music, even if they had very different tastes. His dad was a fan of classic rock, and the pair would blast out The Rolling Stones, Fleetwood Mac, Queen and Pink Floyd from the car radio as they drove around together. Back at home, Harry's mum introduced him to pop, while Gemma played anything and everything from speakers in her bedroom.

For a short time, his mum owned a pub, and the sound of live bands playing late into the night kept little Harry up! He soon got used to the noise though and enjoyed getting to know the musicians. One regular even started teaching him how to play guitar.

Born to Perform

Harry was a born entertainer. His first starring role came aged five, when he took the lead part in a school play – performing as Barney the mouse! For his cute costume, he borrowed Gemma's tights and put on a pair of mouse ears.

Harry would stand in front of his mirror, playing air-guitar along to the music drifting down from his sister's bedroom and pretending to entertain a huge crowd. One year, Harry's grandad bought him a karaoke set. Harry spent hours recording himself singing along to tracks by music legends including Elvis Presley. It looks like practice made perfect as he was cast as the pharaoh in his school's productions of *Joseph and the Amazing Technicolor Dreamcoat* – a character inspired by Elvis!

PRESSING PAUSE

Once he got to secondary school, however, Harry stopped auditioning for plays and stepped out of the spotlight. He still loved to sing – but his talent remained undiscovered as he continued to practise in his bedroom or singing in the shower. Harry liked hanging out with his friends at school, but he found a few subjects tricky. Luckily, Gemma was on hand to help him out with his homework.

HARD-WORKING
Harry

As soon as he was old enough, Harry got himself a part-time job doing a paper round. After a couple of years, he traded his paper round in for a weekend job at a local bakery. He had to get up at 5 a.m. for his shift, where he was put to work slicing bread, washing dishes, unloading boxes and cleaning up the shop. There were some perks, though – Harry occasionally got to eat the cakes that were damaged or burnt!

Today, visitors flock from all around the world to visit the bakery where Harry once worked. The shop has a life-sized poster of Harry, along with a picture of all the One Direction members on display.

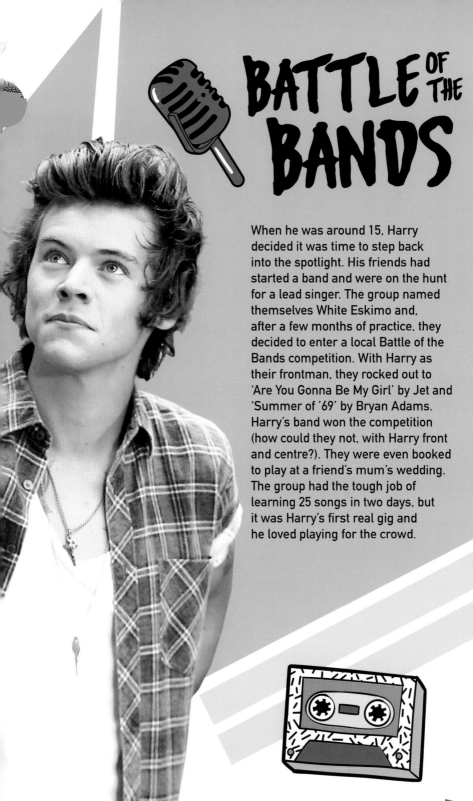

BATTLE OF THE BANDS

When he was around 15, Harry decided it was time to step back into the spotlight. His friends had started a band and were on the hunt for a lead singer. The group named themselves White Eskimo and, after a few months of practice, they decided to enter a local Battle of the Bands competition. With Harry as their frontman, they rocked out to 'Are You Gonna Be My Girl' by Jet and 'Summer of '69' by Bryan Adams. Harry's band won the competition (how could they not, with Harry front and centre?). They were even booked to play at a friend's mum's wedding. The group had the tough job of learning 25 songs in two days, but it was Harry's first real gig and he loved playing for the crowd.

Looking to the Future

Until White Eskimo, Harry hadn't really been sure what he wanted to do after school. He thought about becoming a lawyer and chose some A-levels that would help him get into university. But his real dream was a career in performing – he just wasn't sure how to make it happen. So, when his mum announced she'd sent in an application for Harry to appear on *The X Factor*, Harry was up for trying out!

For all his confidence on stage with White Eskimo, he was nervous about letting his mum and sister hear him practise for his a capella audition – he had to sing without any music, just his voice!

THE X FACTOR

The television singing competition first appeared on our screens way back in 2004 and has now been running for a whopping 15 seasons! It's split into several stages, including auditions, bootcamp, judges' houses and live shows, and the prize is usually a recording contract. It's launched the careers of huge stars including Leona Lewis, Little Mix, James Arthur, JLS, Olly Murs and, of course, One Direction.

AMBITION AND AUDITIONS

Before he even got on the TV show, Harry had to go to an audition at a huge stadium, queuing for hours until it was his turn to sing. After getting through that round, Harry was called back for yet another off-screen audition. He then had an agonizing wait to find out if he'd made it through to the TV show stage. Of course, with that much talent, it was hardly surprising he went through!

Finally, the day arrived when he'd be put to the test in front of judges Simon Cowell, Louis Walsh and Nicole Scherzinger – along with a large live audience! His whole family showed up to support him, wearing T-shirts proudly bearing the slogan 'We Think Harry's Got *The X Factor*'.

With his cute curls and million-dollar smile, Harry charmed the nation and two-thirds of the judges, nailing his performance of 'Isn't She Lovely' by Stevie Wonder. The only judge left unconvinced was Louis, who announced that he didn't think Harry had enough experience or confidence. Despite Louis' doubts, Harry was put through to the next round.

THE END OF THE ROAD

Even after his great start, it almost all ended in tears for Harry. At the end of bootcamp, the judges gathered all the male solo contestants and read out the list of names of those going through to the next stage of the competition. Shockingly, Harry's name wasn't on it! Four other now well-known names were also left off the list… Harry was heartbroken – it seemed his dreams were being dashed before they'd even begun.

But the judges had a surprise in store. They called the names of five boys that hadn't made it through, inviting them back to the stage – this time, Harry's name was one of them! Liam Payne, Louis Tomlinson, Niall Horan and Zayn Malik were also called back. The judges explained that they weren't sure the boys were strong enough as solo artists but felt like they had too much talent to let them go. They were offering them another shot at the competition – but as a group!

A Boy Band is Born

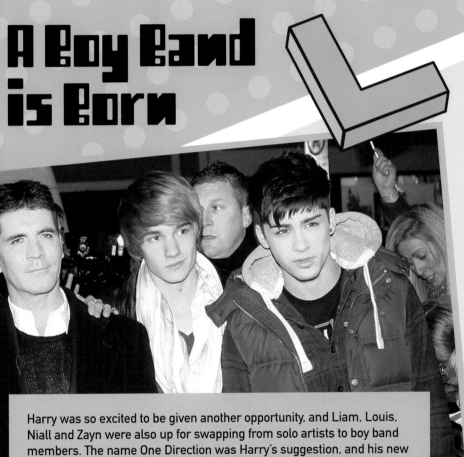

Harry was so excited to be given another opportunity, and Liam, Louis, Niall and Zayn were also up for swapping from solo artists to boy band members. The name One Direction was Harry's suggestion, and his new bandmates quickly got on board. They all went to stay at Harry's dad's house for a couple of weeks to practise singing together. It was a chance for the group to become friends, too, and they spent a lot of time between rehearsals playing football and messing about around a campfire.

Soon, it was back to their duties for *The X Factor*. They flew out to join Simon Cowell at his home in Marbella, Spain, and began preparing for their first performance together.

TV STARS

During the live shows, One Direction (1D) wowed audiences each week, covering hits by Kelly Clarkson, Coldplay and the Beatles. Offstage, they had fun sharing a room in *The X Factor* house and getting to know each other – though it wasn't long before the boys discovered each other's annoying habits, including that Harry was a snorer!

In just a few short weeks, the 1D members transformed from normal teenagers into superstars. After their very first live performance, over two hundred fans waited at the gates of the television studio, desperate to get a glimpse of their new favourite band. Little did the boys know, soon there would be THOUSANDS of fans following them wherever they went.

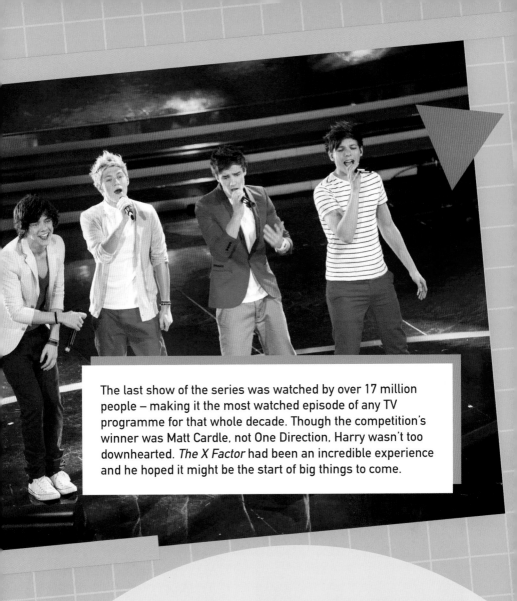

The last show of the series was watched by over 17 million people — making it the most watched episode of any TV programme for that whole decade. Though the competition's winner was Matt Cardle, not One Direction, Harry wasn't too downhearted. *The X Factor* had been an incredible experience and he hoped it might be the start of big things to come.

AFTER *THE X FACTOR*

Sure enough, just a month after the show had finished, One Direction got a record deal with Simon Cowell's label, Syco. Even though they may not have won *The X Factor*, their loyal fans were determined to make them the biggest boy band in the world. Starting in the UK, fans shared their love for Harry, Liam, Louis, Niall and Zayn on Twitter, YouTube and every other platform they could! Before the band had even released any music, they had a worldwide following.

One Direction:

FAST FACTS

LIVE WHILE WE'RE YOUNG

Harry is the youngest member of the group. When the band formed, he'd only just turned 16! Niall and Liam were also 16, Zayn was 17 and, at 18 years old, Louis was the grandad of the group.

ID DON'T DANCE

None of the boys have any dance training and were clear from the start that they didn't want to do dance routines. Or wear matching outfits. They might have been a boy band, but they were going to be a COOL boy band.

FOOT FAIL

1D's first ever TV performance nearly didn't happen. While staying at Simon Cowell's house, Louis had to be rushed to hospital after treading on a spiky sea urchin! Fortunately, he got back in time for the band to prove to Simon that he'd made the right choice keeping them in the competition.

SLOW COACH

While filming the scene in the 'What Makes You Beautiful' music video where Louis drives a campervan along coastal roads, the boys were pulled over by police – twice – for driving too slowly.

GIVING BACK

In 2013, 1D's charity single 'Teenage Kicks (One Way Or Another)' raised over £1 million for Comic Relief. Rather than filming an expensive music video, the boys made the video themselves while on tour.

SECRET SESSIONS

On their final two world tours, 1D's team converted an old surveillance van into a recording studio. The van followed the tour bus around so the group could record their albums in between shows. The worst thing? The van didn't have any air conditioning!

Discover

ONE DIRECTION

LOUIS

Name: Louis Tomlinson
Date of birth: 24 December 1991
Born in: Doncaster, England
Known as: the funny one

Louis always loved performing and was inspired to apply for *The X Factor* after playing Danny in a school production of *Grease*.

Of all the One Direction members, Louis has credits on the most songs — he had a hand in writing 38 of the band's hits.

LIFE AFTER 1D

After One Direction went on hiatus, Louis returned to *The X Factor* as a guest judge in 2018 and became the mentor for the 'Boys' category. Dalton Harris, the winner of the competition, was from Louis' group, making Louis the first former contestant to win the competition as a judge! He's also released a solo album, Walls, and a catchy top-ten hit 'Back to You'. In 2016, he welcomed his baby son, Freddie, to the world, and has loved becoming a father.

LIAM

Name: Liam Payne
Date of birth: 29 August 1993
Born in: Wolverhampton, England
Known as: the responsible one

The series One Direction formed wasn't the first time Liam auditioned for *The X Factor*. Two years earlier, he made it through to the judges' houses stage of the competition, before being eliminated.

Liam said that, had he not auditioned for *The X Factor*, he'd probably have worked in a local aircraft factory, like his dad.

LIFE AFTER 1D

Like the other 1D members, Liam has been using the hiatus to work on new music. His single 'Strip That Down', which came out in 2017, spent almost thirty weeks in the charts. Liam's first solo album, LP1, was released in 2019.

Despite being busy making music, Liam has also found time to start a family. In 2017, Liam and former *The X Factor* judge Cheryl had a baby son, who they named Bear Grey Payne. Though Cheryl and Liam have since split up, they work together to coparent baby Bear.

NIALL

Name: Niall Horan
Date of birth: 13 September 1993
Born in: Mullingar, Ireland
Known as: the cute one

Niall is sports mad! He played golf, football and Gaelic football while he was growing up, and still loves to watch sport today.

A wannabe popstar from a young age, Niall joined his school choir to get in some early practice.

LIFE AFTER 1D

Niall has had a packed schedule since One Direction parted ways, releasing two albums and setting out on a worldwide tour. He's had two amazing singles, 'This Town' and 'Slow Hands', make the top ten. Niall's enjoyed experimenting with his sound and his solo songs have more of a chilled, folky vibe than 1D's pop anthems. Outside of making music, Niall has used his passion for sports to start a golf management company.

ZAYN

Name: Zayn Malik
Date of birth: 12 January 1993
Born in: Bradford, England
Known as: the mysterious one

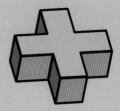

The 1D singer's name was originally spelled 'Zain', but he swapped out the 'i' for a 'y' when auditioning for *The X Factor*, as he preferred the way the word looked.

Zayn almost left *The X Factor* early! He was so nervous about performing a dance number in front of the judges that he slunk off backstage, refusing to perform. Luckily for 1D fans everywhere, Simon Cowell had a quick word and Zayn was convinced to give the choreography a shot.

LIFE AFTER 1D

Since leaving One Direction, Zayn has been able to express his love of R&B music through his two solo albums *Mind of Mine* and *Icarus Falls*. His incredible debut single, 'Pillowtalk' reached the top of the charts in 2016. In September 2020, Zayn and his girlfriend, model Gigi Hadid, welcomed their baby daughter to the world.

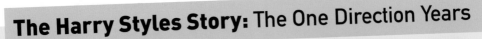
FINDING THEIR FEET

Harry was now part of one of the hottest up-and-coming bands on the planet. The five small-town boys had to grow up fast! Their mums and dads were no longer washing their clothes or cooking their dinners. One Direction were out in the big wide world, dealing with industry experts and the media every day.

Their sound and their style were changing too. Out went singing in unison and scruffy jeans; in came complicated harmonies and fashion-forward outfits. Even if the boys didn't dance, they were certainly learning to command a stage!

A FIRST SINGLE

'What Makes You Beautiful', One Direction's first single, hit the airwaves in September 2011. The track shot to number one in the UK and sold nearly five million copies worldwide. The hit also found success in the States when it was released a few months later. In the past, British boy bands had struggled to make it big across the pond, but 1D's very first single rocketed into the top ten. Not since the Beatles had a band from the UK become so internationally huge. The fun-packed video for 'What Makes You Beautiful' featured the group messing around at the beach. Harry and the others had a blast filming their first music video – even if Zayn did bury Harry in the sand when he was taking a quick kip!

Time on

When their first album *Up All Night* was released, it topped the charts in sixteen countries. In the space of a year, One Direction had gone from third place to top of the world. The group took their first album on tour, performing 62 shows, and even expanded their route to include North America, Australia and New Zealand.

One of Harry's favourite things about the tour was getting to spend time on their tour bus. Here, he could relax after shows, play video games, chat to his family over the phone and catch up on sleep. He also loved seeing the world – Sydney, New York and Los Angeles were three of his favourite cities.

Harry might be an international heartthrob, but he doesn't let the fame get to his head. He hates the word 'famous' and lives by the motto 'Work hard, play hard and be kind.'

Tour

STAYING GROUNDED

Even though he'd never even visited London before
The X Factor, he decided to buy a house in the capital.
While it was being renovated, he slept in the attic
bedroom of a friend's house. It was hardly a rock-and-
roll lifestyle – after performing to crowds of thousands
of people, Harry would have to sneak up the stairs to
his little room, so as not to disturb his hosts!

HEADING BACK HOME

Harry loved being on tour, making amazing music videos and recording awesome albums, but the busy schedule did take its toll. Whenever he got the chance, Harry went back to Holmes Chapel to spend time with his family. The normality of having tea on the table, of being able to take a three-hour nap without his alarm buzzing, of chatting with his mum about all the crazy stuff going on around him, gave Harry strength. He didn't even mind doing a few jobs around the house!

In 2013, Harry's mum remarried and Harry was best man at the wedding. He said that giving a speech was one of the most nerve-wracking things he'd ever done.

Bigger and Better

One Direction continued on their mission for world domination, releasing bestselling single after bestselling single. They followed up *Up All Night* with two more chart-topping albums *Take Me Home* and *Midnight Memories*. Harry's schedule was always jam-packed – he'd often go straight from the recording studio to the stage, then back to the recording studio, with hardly any time to sleep or eat in between!

1D toured the world and performed at some pretty amazing events, including at Madison Square Garden in New York, the London 2012 Olympic closing ceremony and the Royal Variety Performance in front of Queen Elizabeth II. They picked up nearly 200 awards along the way, including their very first BRIT for best single in 2012.

This is US

In 2013, Harry, Liam, Louis, Niall and Zayn took their fans behind the scenes in documentary *This is Us*. The film showed the world the silly side of One Direction as the boys mucked around backstage at stadiums, but also their sweet side, as they spent time with their fans and returned home to visit their families. Though the boys worked hard, it was clear they played hard, too.

The teen idols were growing up. They were no longer floppy-haired schoolboys, but young men with a distinct sound and image. And it was often Harry who the fans screamed the loudest for!

COPING WITH FAME

Harry sometimes struggled with the paparazzi. It was hard to deal with all the flashing cameras in his face and the silly, or even nasty, rumours in the press. He couldn't even go on a date with Taylor Swift in Central Park without the whole world knowing about it. Although he loved his fans, walking into a room full of people screaming at him was hard to get used to as well. Having such amazing friends and family around him was really important to Harry and helped him cope with the intense bits of his new life.

THEN THERE

After the release of their fourth album and during their fourth world tour, 1D made an announcement that shocked the world. Zayn had decided it was time for him to leave the band behind. He wanted to take a step back from the spotlight and focus on other areas of his life. Though Harry was shocked his friend wanted to leave, he respected Zayn's decision. It was up to him, Liam, Louis and Niall to be there for their fans and finish the tour.

WE'RE FOUR

Saying Goodbye

After Zayn left, Harry became even closer to his remaining bandmates as they worked out how to make the group work as a four-piece. Even though their fifth member was massively missed, the four remaining boys worked incredibly hard to create even more amazing music. They released 'Drag Me Down' in July 2015, then followed it up with their fifth and final album, *Made in the AM*.

They'd spent five incredible years together, travelled across the world and topped the charts in countless countries. At the end of 2015, Harry and the band made a difficult decision. They decided it was time for them to go on an 'indefinite hiatus' – a break with no fixed end date. They weren't officially splitting up, but it was unclear when, or even if, they would get back together. "To you who support us, in any way, thank you," Harry tweeted after the announcement. "We wouldn't be here without you. You did this and we thank you for having us. All the love."

Their final live show was in Sheffield on 31 October 2015, and it was an emotional performance. As the show drew to a close, Harry hugged his bandmates and thanked their fans, once again, for everything they'd done.

DIRECTIONERS

Are you a Directioner? Around the world, One Direction's followers are some of the loyalest, loudest and most passionate fans in the world! 1D's fame, success and good times are all thanks to their fantastic fan base.

From packing out stadiums to spreading the love on social media, Directioners took the boys all the way to the top – and the members of 1D loved giving back! From snapping thousands of selfies to recording video messages, scribbling their autographs on anything and everything to helping fans propose to their partners, Harry, Liam, Louis, Niall and Zayn loved being there for their fans' special moments.

Fans sometimes go too far, however. After poor Harry was sick at the side of the road in LA, fans set up a little shrine to him, with a poster reading "Harry Styles Threw Up Here". Yuck!

These days, Harry's so used to fans throwing presents at him on stage that he's developed a kind of sixth sense, and often catches the gift grenades! (DO NOT try this though – throwing things at performers is NOT cool. It could get you chucked out of the venue or, worse, hurt the artist.)

2013
OMER
RE !
1D

Please come
and
1D say 'hello' 1D

PROUD OF
ONE
DIRECTION
3 YEARS OF 1D   JULY 23rd

EXPE

Imagine you are at a One Direction concert, or in the audience at one of Harry's solo shows. What does your sign say?

1D in Numbers

During their five years together, One Direction smashed records and made history. Here are the facts and stats to prove it.

16

The number of countries their debut album, *Up All Night*, topped the charts in.

175 MILLION

The combined number of Twitter followers the 1D boys have. The band's official account still has a following of 31.5 million, even without any new music for over five years.

10.9 MILLION

The number of views the video for 'Best Song Ever' got in 24 hours back in 2013.

300,000

The number of tickets sold for 1D's *Take Me Home* Tour, within a day of them being released.

7

The number of BRIT Awards the band has received over the years, including four trophies for Best British Video. They've also picked up six Billboard Awards, four MTV Video Music Awards and had a whopping 28 wins at the Teen Choice Awards.

70 MILLION

The number of records the band sold as of April 2020.

3.4 MILLION

The number of fans that attended the 69 shows of their *Where We Are* Tour.

6

The number of times One Direction appear in the *Guinness World Records*, 2015 edition. One of the records they smashed was becoming the first band from the UK to have a debut album enter at number one in the charts in the United States.

1

The number of times Directioners won a Radio Disney Music Award for Fiercest Fans!

TAKING A STEP BACK

After the band went on hiatus, Harry took a bit of time to catch his breath. He visited friends and family, and started trying to figure out what he wanted to do next.

In July 2016, the announcement came that Harry had signed a solo record deal. Fans couldn't wait to hear what he came up with. Would he stick to what he knew, creating catchy pop tunes like One Direction, or would his solo sound be very different? All the world could do was wait and see.

A Different Spotlight

Harry had hardly begun working on his first solo album when he put in on pause. An opportunity had come up to try something totally different. Director Christopher Nolan was holding auditions for a film called *Dunkirk*, a drama about soldiers evacuating from the beaches of France during World War Two. Christopher was impressed with his acting talent (even though Harry hadn't acted properly since primary school). He offered Harry the part of a young soldier called Alex.

Filming was physically tough – Harry's character is in a sinking ship for most of the movie, so he spent his days waist-deep in cold water with sand in his eyes. Perhaps toughest of all was the fact he had to cut off his curly locks for the role! It was all worth it though – the film was a success, with fans and critics praising Harry's acting debut.

MAKING Music Magic

After filming was finished, Harry got down to the business of making his first solo record. "I really wanted to make an album that I wanted to listen to," he said. "That was the only way I knew I wouldn't look back on it and regret it." He swapped the chilly waters of France for the warm beaches of Jamaica, working with his team from dusk until dawn. Harry lived and breathed music, admitting he even went a little island crazy. Long days would be spent in the studio, followed by evenings swimming in the sea. Harry would sometimes stay up late into the night watching rom-coms!

Harry wanted his album to be honest; he wanted to be truthful with his fans, as well as with himself. Between them, the team created around thirty songs, which they narrowed down to the ten final tracks on the album. Harry was inspired by lots of artists and genres from the past, but he wanted to create something that was very much of the moment, too. Harry had found a sound totally his own — and he was ready to share it with the world.

A SIGN OF THE TIMES

Harry's first solo single 'Sign of the Times' came out in April 2017. He definitely hadn't played it safe – the song was a seven-minute ballad, with powerful lyrics and a soft-rock sound. There is even a moving backstory to the song: it's "written from a point of view as if a mother was giving birth to a child and there's a complication. The mother is told, 'The child is fine, but you're not going to make it.' The mother has five minutes to tell the child, 'Go forth and conquer.'"

Hope you're not afraid of heights, Harry! When the idea for the 'Sign of the Times' video was first pitched to Harry, the director said he'd be hanging from a rope attached to a helicopter, around twenty feet (six metres) above the ground. As the day of filming approached, the proposed height kept getting higher and higher. Harry ended up being suspended 1,500 feet (457 metres) above the ground! He spent the whole time thinking "I can't wait to get down!"

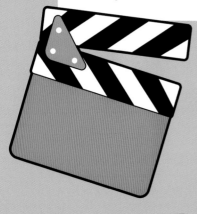

MOMENT OF TRUTH

Before it was released, Harry played the album to his family. His mum was so moved by a couple of the tracks that she burst into tears! His stepdad, on the other hand, simply asked one question about the song 'Woman': "How did you get a duck in the studio?" There was no duck – the sound he was talking about was just Harry singing!

In May 2017, Harry Styles released his self-titled album. As if there was ever any doubt, it went straight to the top of the charts. It even got the highest first-week sales in the United States by any British male solo artist EVER. Music magazine *Rolling Stone* declared Harry had claimed "his turf as a true rock-and-roll prince".

SETTING OUT SOLO

In summer 2017, Harry set off on his very first solo tour, taking in 25 countries and 88 venues. He mixed up his set by including 1D tracks and few covers, as well as performing the songs from his new album. Harry treated fans to a new style, as well as new songs, wearing a different, colourful suit for each show!

At every performance, Harry told his fans it was a space where they could "be whoever it is you chose to be". He showed his love and support for members of the LGBTQ+ community by waving a rainbow flag at some of his shows, and spread a heart-warming message of love, acceptance and kindness. He'd officially become a rock star.

Beyond the Music

Having proven to the world that he could be a successful solo artist, Harry took a short break from making music and touring. Still he kept busy, helping James Corden present *The Late Late Show*, modelling for Gucci and even co-hosting the most stylish event of the year, the Met Gala.

Second Album

SUCCESS

It wasn't long before Harry was back in the studio though. In some ways, he felt the pressure was off. He already had a successful first solo album under his belt, so could be even more open and experimental in his second record. Harry had gone through a lot in his personal life in the last couple of years – break-ups and make-ups, love found and love lost. He poured his emotions into his music, letting the album flip between the catchy highs of 'Watermelon Sugar' to the hushed lows of 'Falling'.

Harry's second album, *Fine Line*, came out in December 2019. Its colourful album cover featured a photo of Harry through a fisheye lens, wearing a pink shirt and white wide-legged trousers – it was an album with a difference, with something for everyone. It hit the number one spot in 12 countries and was even nominated for Album of the Year at the BRIT Awards.

What Next?

As the coronavirus pandemic swept across the planet in 2020, like lots of people, Harry had to put his plans on hold. He was due to set out on a second solo world tour, but had to postpone it by a year in order to keep his crew and fans safe. Poor Harry ended up getting stuck self-isolating in LA, unable to get home to London. Still, he made the most of the time, practising musical instruments, reading lots of books and FaceTiming his family.

As for what the future holds for Harry Styles? Who knows – but it's bound to be something exciting. From making new music, to appearing in more movies (he's rumoured to be starring in a psychological thriller in 2022), to wowing the world with his bold fashion choices, it's exciting to think that Harry is only just getting started. As for a 1D reunion, well, as Harry says – "I don't think I'd ever say I'd never do it again, because I don't feel that way. If there's a time when we all really want to do it, that's the only time for us to do it." Fingers crossed!

Harry's HEROES

Harry's been a big music fan ever since he was a little boy, but his music taste is wide-ranging. Here are a few of his favourite artists from the past.

The Beatles

Harry grew up listening to the sixties rock band whose legendary tracks include 'Hey Jude', 'Yesterday' and 'Let It Be'. Like One Direction, the Beatles had a very dedicated fan base – the hype surrounding the famous four-piece became known as Beatlemania. Harry's a particularly big fan of Paul McCartney's song-writing skills.

Stevie Nicks

Fleetwood Mac singer Stevie Nicks has long been a hero of Harry's – and the respect is mutual. Stevie has called Harry her "little muse" and the pair have performed some incredible duets together.

Van Morrison

The Irish rock star's album *Astral Weeks* is one of Harry's favourite records of all time. When Harry met his hero backstage, the pair posed for a photo together. Harry tickled Van to get him to smile in the pic!

Shania Twain

One of his mum's favourite artists, Harry has said he's inspired by both Shania's style and her music. 'You're Still the One' by the Canadian singer is one of Harry's favourite songs ever written. There are even rumours of an upcoming collaboration!

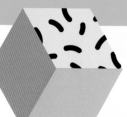

Elvis Presley

Legendary entertainer Elvis is the original "King of Rock and Roll". Harry used to listen to Elvis's records at his grandparents' house and even put together a tape of Elvis covers for his grandad. One side of the tape had Elvis hits, but the other had Eminem covers – and Harry ended up playing his grandad the wrong side!

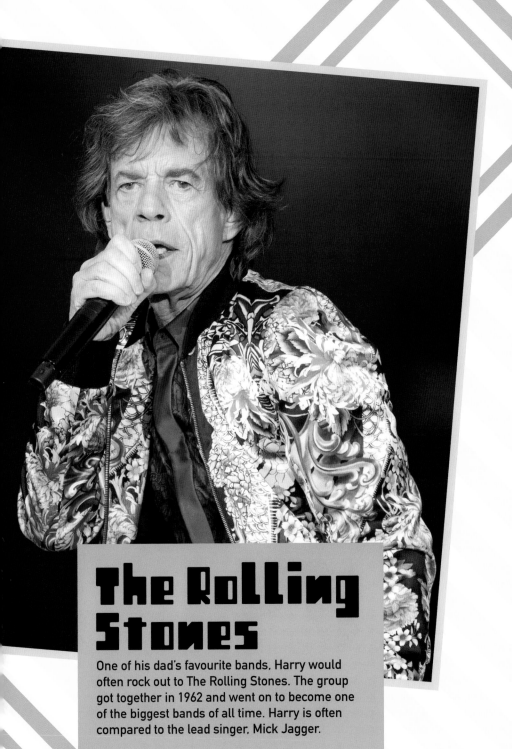

The Rolling Stones

One of his dad's favourite bands, Harry would often rock out to The Rolling Stones. The group got together in 1962 and went on to become one of the biggest bands of all time. Harry is often compared to the lead singer, Mick Jagger.

What's Your HARRY STYLES HIT?

Discover which Harry Styles song most suits your personality in this flow chart quiz.

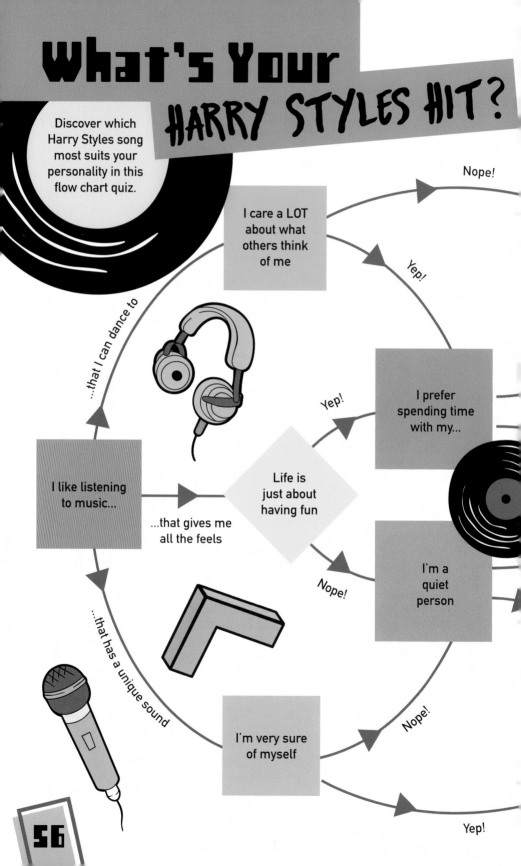

I care a LOT about what others think of me

Nope!

Yep!

...that I can dance to

I like listening to music...

...that gives me all the feels

Life is just about having fun

Yep!

I prefer spending time with my...

Nope!

I'm a quiet person

...that has a unique sound

I'm very sure of myself

Nope!

Yep!

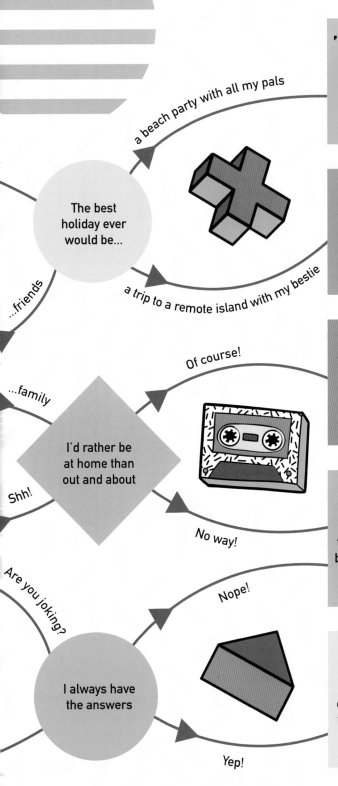

·WATERMELON SUGAR·
You are the life and soul of the party! You just love being around people and having a good time.

·ADORE YOU·
You'd do anything for your friends! You are a loyal and caring person with a lot of love to give.

·SWEET CREATURE·
You're a gentle soul who likes the simple things in life. You'd rather be cozied up at home than out and about.

·LIGHTS UP·
You're totally unique! Remember, it's okay not to know who you want to be or what you want to do yet. That's what growing up is about!

·SIGN OF THE TIMES·
Serious and thoughtful, you're the person everyone seems to come to for advice. Remember to step back from it all sometimes and relax!

a beach party with all my pals

The best holiday ever would be...

a trip to a remote island with my bestie

...friends

...family

Shh!

Of course!

I'd rather be at home than out and about

No way!

Are you joking?

Nope!

I always have the answers

Yep!

FAMOUS FRIENDS

Harry's rubbed shoulders with an impressively long list of celebrities. His phone must be full of famous numbers!

ED SHEERAN

Harry and world-famous singer-songwriter Ed go way back. They were friends even before Ed gave One Direction his song 'Little Things' for their second album. They even have matching tattoos – Harry has the word 'Pingu' inked near his armpit and Ed has a little drawing of the TV penguin.

LIZZO

Lizzo and Harry's friendship is just too cute! This pair of musical powerhouses have performed Lizzo's hit 'Juice' together and have a lot of love for each other. Harry has a lot of respect for Lizzo – he admires how she's not afraid to be herself.

CARA DELEVINGNE

After these pair were spotted going to the theatre together and attending a fashion show, rumours that they were dating began to circulate. But Harry's always been clear that he and Cara are just good friends.

KENDALL JENNER

Reality TV star and supermodel Kendall Jenner is another one of Harry's close friends. Harry and Kendall dated for a while but remained pals after the relationship ended.

JAMES CORDEN

The actor-turned-TV-show-host is a true Directioner and admits he was a little bit heartbroken when the band broke up. He and Harry are very close and have been there for each other both personally and professionally. Harry has appeared on James's TV show, *The Late Late Show*, heaps of times.

HARRY'S FRIENDSHIP TIP #02
Be kind to people and think about their feelings. "You have a choice where you can either be all right to someone or you can be a little bit nicer, and that can make someone's day."

ADELE

Superstar Adele and Harry met through the world of showbiz. Adele gave Harry a copy of her album *21* for his twenty-first birthday!

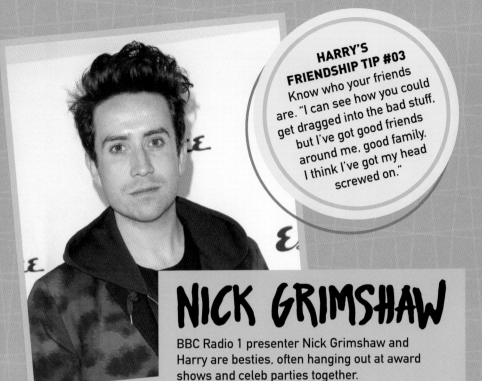

HARRY'S
FRIENDSHIP TIP #03
Know who your friends
are. "I can see how you could
get dragged into the bad stuff,
but I've got good friends
around me, good family.
I think I've got my head
screwed on."

NICK GRIMSHAW

BBC Radio 1 presenter Nick Grimshaw and Harry are besties, often hanging out at award shows and celeb parties together.

LIAM, NIALL ZAYN AND LOUIS

The 1D boys may have parted ways professionally but they'll always be an important part of each other's lives. July 2020 marked One Direction's ten-year anniversary and Harry tweeted his love for his boy band brothers and all the amazing times they'd shared together.

Living in the spotlight has its drawbacks and the media snooping into your love life is one of them. Harry tries to keep a low profile when going on dates as he wants to keep his relationships as private as possible. Unfortunately, when you're as famous as Harry, it's hard to keep a budding romance a secret for long!

Harry's Hobbies

Harry's schedule is often so jam-packed that he has little time to relax and enjoy himself. When he gets the chance, he loves to keep fit, catch up with his friends and explore new places.

Reading

Growing up, Harry wasn't much of a reader, but in recent years he's started to enjoy getting stuck into a good book. Some of his favourite authors include Japanese writer Haruki Murakami and German-American writer Charles Bukowski.

Travelling

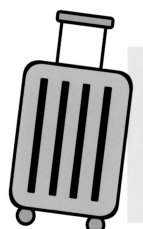

While he may have travelled the world on multiple tours, Harry rarely had the opportunity to do any sightseeing. Before making his second album, he jetted off to one of his favourite cities, Tokyo, and spent a whole month exploring on his own.

Working Out

Keeping fit is important for a superstar with a gruelling schedule, but as well as cardio workouts, Harry enjoys slower-paced classes, including yoga and pilates.

Journalling

Harry keeps a journal that he tries to write in regularly – even if it's just a quick note or a couple of bullet points so he remembers how amazing an experience was.

Making a Difference

As well as having fun trying new hobbies, Harry uses his fame to do good. On a rare day off in LA, Harry drove around the city handing out pizzas to people living on the streets.

STYLE ICON

Harry's come a long way since he auditioned for *The X Factor* wearing a cardigan and a skinny scarf. He's transformed into a worldwide fashion icon, with a sophisticated wardrobe of incredible looks.

In November 2020, Harry made history by becoming the first-ever male cover star of *Vogue* in the US.

Harry enjoys experimenting with fashion. Harry believes people should be free to wear whatever they like. As he told one journalist: "If I see a nice shirt and get told, 'But it's for ladies.' I think: Okaaaay? Doesn't make me want to wear it less though…"

From brightly coloured fingernails to sparkling rings, pearl necklaces to chic bags, Harry knows how to complete a look!

"I LOVE AN ACCESSORY AS MUCH AS THE NEXT PERSON."
Harry Styles

Harry's favourite designers include Gucci and Burberry.

Suit Up, Look Sharp

Try your hand at fashion design and doodle a stylish new suit for Harry's next performance.

Now draw some awesome accessories to go with the dazzling new outfit that you've designed for Harry.

Harry has over fifty tattoos, including a couple he's even inked on himself!

Lots of Harry's tattoos are inspired by the kind of old-fashioned designs that were popular with sailors years ago, including an anchor, a mermaid and a pair of swallows.

Harry's HAIR

This wouldn't be a Harry Styles fan book without a celebration of the superstar's incredible locks. Here's a timeline of Harry's hairstyles over the years.

2010 FLOPPY MOP
Harry auditioned for *The X Factor* with a sweet, just-got-out-of-bed hairstyle.

2012 CUTE CURLS
Harry's curly hair made him a favourite among Directioners.

2013 HARRY'S HEADBANDS
With his curls growing out, Harry often swept back his longer locks using an oversized headband.

2014

SWEPT BACK STYLE
Headbands became a thing of the past as Harry let his hair grow into a casual and cool style.

2016

LONG AND LUSCIOUS
The most rock star of Harry's looks, these long tresses helped Harry stand out from the crowd.

2017

CHOPPED AND COIFFED
After snipping off his hair for his role in *Dunkirk*, Harry started to sweep it back in a new, slicker style.

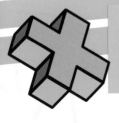

2019

CURLS COMEBACK
Harry's signature curls reappear, much to his fans' delight!

LOST IN THE LYRICS

Music is where Harry lets the lines between his public life and private life blur. Through his lyrics, he explores real-life experiences, from falling in love to having his heart broken. Use these pages to have a go at writing your own verses – you might find it therapeutic, like Harry!

If you're stuck, don't worry about forcing rhymes or coming up with clever lines, just write about how you feel, at this very moment.

Find Your Voice

If you want to follow in Harry's footsteps and become a singing sensation, you'll need to work for it – and work hard. Discover some top tips for achieving your dreams.

PRACTICE MAKES PERFECT

Just like Harry with his childhood karaoke machine, you have to put in the practice to get really good at something. Singing talent will take you so far, but your performance style is important, too. Whether it's performing in front of a group of trusted friends or your mum, don't be too shy to show off those skills!

KNOW YOUR STRENGTHS...

You can't be good at absolutely everything – even Harry admits he's not the world's greatest dancer. Perhaps you struggle to reach high notes or find it hard to harmonize. Maybe you're better in a group than singing solo? Get to know your strengths and work on your weaknesses, so you can become the best possible version of yourself.

...BUT PUSH YOUR LIMITS

There's nothing wrong with sticking to what you know, but you don't want to play it safe all the time. Try new styles of music, cover songs in different genres and collaborate with friends. Until you push yourself, you'll never know how far you can go.

TREAT PEOPLE WITH KINDNESS

You don't have to be cut-throat or catty to get to the top. Focus on building yourself up, rather than tearing others down. Follow in Harry's footsteps, spreading love, joy and laughter wherever you go!

HOW WELL DO YOU KNOW Harry?

So, you reckon you're the ultimate Harry Styles fan? Try this tricky quiz to discover how well you know the new prince of pop. Circle your answers then turn to page 77 to discover your score.

1 WHAT IS HARRY'S SISTER'S NAME?

a) Jenna
b) Gemma
c) Jenny
d) Jessica

2 WHAT WAS HARRY'S WEEKEND JOB WHEN HE WAS A TEENAGER?

a) He washed cars at a garage
b) He babysat for his next-door neighbours
c) He helped out at the local bakery
d) He was a lifeguard at a swimming pool

3 WHAT WAS THE NAME OF HARRY'S BAND AT SCHOOL?

a) Pink Snowflake
b) Silver Snowman
c) Black Blizzard
d) White Eskimo

4 WHAT SONG DID HARRY SING AT HIS FIRST (FILMED) *THE X FACTOR* AUDITION?

a) 'Let Me Love You' by Mario
b) 'Hey There Delilah' by Plain White T's
c) 'Isn't She Lovely' by Stevie Wonder
d) 'Cry Me a River' by Michael Bublé

5 COMPLETE THE LYRICS FROM ONE DIRECTION'S HIT 'BEST SONG EVER': SAID HER NAME WAS GEORGIA ROSE / AND HER DADDY WAS A...

a) Hairdresser
b) Butcher
c) Lawyer
d) Dentist

6 WHAT YEAR DID ONE DIRECTION ANNOUNCE THEIR HIATUS?

a) 2013
b) 2015
c) 2017
d) 2019

7 WHICH OF THESE IS NOT A HARRY STYLES SONG?

a) 'Slow Hands'
b) 'Golden'
c) 'Two Ghosts'
d) 'Only Angel'

8 WHAT WAS THE NAME OF HARRY'S CHARACTER IN THE FEATURE FILM *DUNKIRK*?

a) Tom　　b) Jack　　c) Will　　d) Alex

9 IN THE MUSIC VIDEO FOR 'ADORE YOU', WHAT ANIMAL DOES HARRY RESCUE AND KEEP AS A PET?

a) A fish
b) A hamster
c) A dog
d) A tiger

BONUS QUESTION
Do you know the name of the fictional island where the 'Adore You' video was set?

10 ON THE ALBUM COVER FOR FINE LINE, WHAT COLOUR TOP IS HARRY WEARING?

a) Pink
b) White
c) Blue
d) Black

11 WHICH OF THESE FRUITS IS NOT IN THE TITLE OF ONE OF HARRY'S SOLO HITS?

a) Kiwi
b) Watermelon
c) Strawberry
d) Cherry

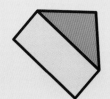

12 WHICH CHILDREN'S TV CHARACTER DOES HARRY HAVE A TATTOO IN TRIBUTE TO?

a) Tinky Winky
b) Pingu
c) Winnie-the-Pooh
d) SpongeBob SquarePants

0-4 HARRY WHO?

So, you may not be too savvy about the life and music of Harry Styles but – don't worry – it's fine to be a casual fan, too.

5-7 RIGHT DIRECTION

Not bad! You clearly know a few things about heartthrob Harry Styles. You could always flick through the book again to fill in those gaps.

8-12 STYLES SUPERFAN

Congratulations, Harry Styles fan, you really know your stuff. If only Harry's car could break down in front of your house!

Bonus question answer: Eroda (which is 'adore' spelled backwards – but of course you knew that!)

1.a; 2.c; 3.d; 4.c; 5.d; 6.b; 7.a; 8.d; 9.a; 10.a; 11.c; 12.b

ANSWERS

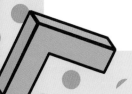

STYLES SCRAPBOOK

"A DREAM IS ONLY A DREAM ... UNTIL YOU DECIDE TO MAKE IT REAL."

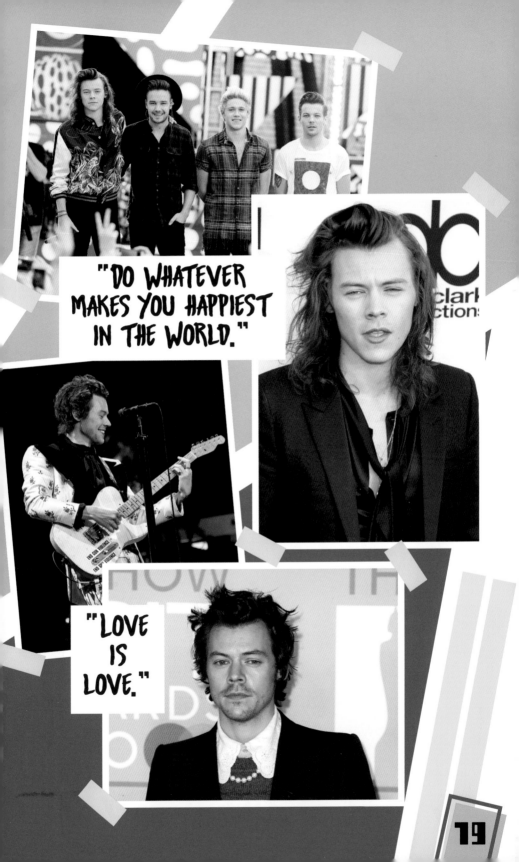

"DO WHATEVER MAKES YOU HAPPIEST IN THE WORLD."

"LOVE IS LOVE."

Picture Credits

While every effort has been made to credit all contributors, we would like to apologize should there be any omissions or errors, and would be pleased to make any appropriate corrections for future editions of this book.

GETTY IMAGES

Front cover image: NBC
Back cover image: Kevin Mazur

P3 NBC; P7, P68b Jeff Kravitz; PP8-9 Handout; PP12-13, P78tr NBC Newswire; P10, P24, P25, P26, P27, P36, 78tl John Furniss; PP18-19, P78b Tony Woolliscroft; PP44-45, P72 James D. Morgan; PP28-29 FilmMagic; PP30-31 Danny Martindale; PP32-33 Johannes Eisele; PP36-37, P79t Stephen Lovekin; PP46-47, P69cl Patricia Schlein/Star Max; P48, P59t, P79cr Kevin Mazur; P49, P64 John Shearer; PP50-51, PP62-63, P65t, P69b Neil Mockford; PP52-53 Theo Wargo; P65br, P79b Gareth Cattermole, P65bl Jason Merritt/TERM; P69t Steve Granitz.

SHUTTERSTOCK.COM

P5, PP14-15 Debby Wong; P6, P42, P60b, P69cr, P79cr Tinseltown; PP10-11, PP34-35, PP38-39, P61, P68t Featureflash Photo Agency; PP20-21, P59b Andrea Raffin; P43 Fokke Baarssen; PP54-55 Shayne Friessner-Day; P58, P60t Cubankite; P59c DFree; P68c Mr Pics.